Math + Fashion = Fun

**Move to the head of the class with
math puzzles to help you pass!**

by Aubre Andrus

★ American Girl®

Published by American Girl Publishing
Copyright © 2012 by American Girl

Questions or comments? Call 1-800-845-0005, visit americangirl.com,
or write to Customer Service, American Girl, 8400 Fairway Place, Middleton, WI 53562-0497.

Printed in China
12 13 14 15 16 17 18 19 LEO 10 9 8 7 6 5 4 3 2 1

Editorial Development: Carrie Anton
Art Direction and Design: Gretchen Becker
Production: Jeannette Bailey, Kendra Schluter, Tami Kepler, Judith Lary
Illustrations: Thu Thai at Arcana Studios
Picture Credit: © iStockphoto/daveporter (paper money)

Special thanks to Michael Thompson

Dear Reader,

Welcome to Innerstar University! At this imaginary, one-of-a-kind school, you can live with your friends in a dorm called Brightstar House and find lots of fun ways to develop new skills and let your true talents shine.

This book is packed with fun math puzzles, games, and tips. Through things such as secret number codes, arithmetic riddles, and mathematical mazes, you'll learn how to solve problems without a calculator, and you'll pick up a few secrets that help math make more sense. Tucked in the back of this book are cool tools that will help perfect your arithmetic skills.

If you get stuck or just want to check your answers, turn to page 72. Have a good time finding your way through all the puzzles! Then head over to www.innerstarU.com for even more games and fun.

Your friends at American Girl

Innerstar Guides

Every girl needs a few good friends to help her find her way.

Emmy

A brave girl who loves swimming and boating

Isabel

A confident girl with a funky sense of style

Riley

A good sport, on the field and off

Paige

A nature lover who leads hikes and campus cleanups

Amber

An animal lover and a loyal friend

Neely

A creative girl who loves dance, music, and art

Logan

A super-smart girl who is curious about EVERYTHING

Shelby

A kind girl who is there for her friends—and loves making NEW friends!

Innerstar U Campus

1. Rising Star Stables
2. Star Student Center
3. Brightstar House
4. Starlight Library
5. Sparkle Studios
6. Blue Sky Nature Center

7. Real Spirit Center

8. Five-Points Plaza

9. Starfire Lake & Boathouse

10. U-Shine Hall

11. Good Sports Center

12. Shopping Square

13. The Market

14. Morningstar Meadow

Contents

Check it out, then check it off!

☐ Bead Bins 11

☐ Color Coordinated.. 12

☐ Clothing Code 14

☐ Lots to Dot 18

☐ "Hairbrained" Teasers................................... 19

☐ Sock Stock 20

☐ Purse Prediction..22

☐ Slumber Savings 23

☐ Messy Maze 24

☐ Funny Fashion 26

☐ Sequence Sequins...27

☐ Bracelet Bonanza... 28

☐ Loads of Leggings 29

☐ Earring Organizer.. 30

☐ Sweater Stacks 32

☐ Cap Combine 33

☐ Perfect Gift Search 34

☐ Formal Affair 36

☐ Shopping Bag Bundle 37

☐ Hidden Accessories 38

☐ Good Deal... 40

☐ Hair Affair..42

☐ Quick Change 43

☐ Fashion Fractions 44

❏ Spending Stumpers 46

❏ Pendant Count 48

❏ Shoe Pair-Up 49

❏ Fashion Frames 50

❏ Charity Knitting.. 52

❏ Budget Busters 53

❏ Exact Change.. 54

❏ Twisted Tags 56

❏ Design Dots 57

❏ Math Makeover.. 58

❏ Clothing Conundrum.. 60

❏ Bead Blanks.. 62

❏ It All Adds Up 63

❏ Market Maze 64

❏ Message Mix-Up 66

❏ Jewelry Palooza 67

❏ Purchase Path..68

❏ Store Secret.. 70

Answers start on page 72.

Meet Isabel

Work side by side with your Innerstar University guide.

As Innerstar University's math expert, Isabel's the go-to girl for everything related to numbers, equations, and calculations. Oh, and fashion! After all, you can't shop without using a little math, right?

With clothing drives, a jewelry-making business, and shopping for new styles, Isabel needs math every minute of the day! Luckily she has a few secrets up her sleeve. As you solve the fashion-related puzzles and problems in this book, Isabel will teach you a few tricks along the way. With Isabel's creative style, you'll see how much fun it is to deal with decimals, add and subtract big numbers with ease, and calculate answers quickly in your head.

Look for my speech bubbles for tips and guidance throughout the book.

Bead Bins

Isabel and Neely are setting up bead bins so that they can make bracelets quickly and easily. Fill each bin below with a number from 1 to 9 (3, 4, and 8 have been done for you). You can use each number only once! Each row of bins must total 15 when you add in any direction—up and down, side to side, or diagonally.

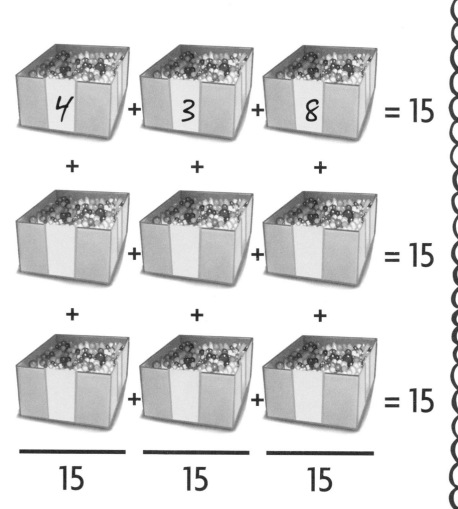

4 + 3 + 8 = 15

+   +   +

+   + = 15

+   +   +

+   + = 15

15   15   15

Color Coordinated

**Solve these problems, and then use the answers
to color in a creative style.**

24 = pink   **20 = purple**   6 = green

12 = blue   40 = yellow

a. 6 x 2 = ____

b. 2 x 3 = ____

c. 5 x 4 = ____

d. 12 x 2 = ____

e. 3 x 2 = ____

f. 48 ÷ 2 = ____

g. 10 x 4 = ____

h. 36 ÷ 6 = ____

i. 8 x 5 = ____

j. 10 x 2 = ____

k. 20 x 2 = ____

l. 4 x 3 = ____

m. 8 x 3 = ____

Clothing Code

Isabel and Neely want to send written messages in code, but they need your help. Solve the problems to complete the decoder. Then turn to page 16 to solve the clothing riddles.

A	B	C	D	E	F	G	H	I	J	K	L	M
17												

N	O	P	Q	R	S	T	U	V	W	X	Y	Z

A.   98
        -81
        ‾‾‾‾
         17

B.   105
        -104
        ‾‾‾‾

C.   72
       ÷ 36
       ‾‾‾‾

D.   7
        + 6
       ‾‾‾‾

E.   64
        ÷16
       ‾‾‾‾

F.   6
        x 3
       ‾‾‾‾

G.   88
        ÷11
       ‾‾‾‾

H.   85
        -62
       ‾‾‾‾

I.   39
        ÷13
       ‾‾‾‾

J.   51
   −32

K.   3
   x 3

L.   70
   ÷10

M.   7
   +7

N.   54
   ÷9

O.   58
   −42

P.   120
   ÷12

Q.   36
   −11

R.   7
   x 3

S.   14
   +12

T.   35
   ÷7

U.   121
   ÷11

V.   8
   x 3

W.   74
   −62

X.   15
   + 5

Y.   45
   ÷3

Z.   19
   +3

Use the decoder from pages 14–15 to crack up from these clothing jokes.

1. What did 0 say to 8?

___ ___ ___ ___   ___ ___ ___ ___
6   3   2   4   1   4   7   5

2. What kind of shoes do spies wear?

___ ___ ___ ___ ___ ___ ___ ___
26 6 4 17 9 4 21 26

3. What has shoulders and a neck but no legs or head?

___   ___ ___ ___ ___ ___
17   26 23 3 21 5

4. What wears a coat in winter and pants all summer?

___   ___ ___ ___
17   13 16 8

5. What are a plumber's favorite shoes?

___ ___ ___ ___ ___
2 7 16 8 26

6. What type of sandals do frogs wear?

___ ___ ___ ___ - ___ ___ ___ ___
16 10 4 6   5 16 17 13

7. How much do pirates pay for their earrings?

___   ___ ___ ___ ___ ___ ___ ___ ___
17   1 11 2 2 17 6 4 4 21

Want to share top-secret messages with your friends? Tear out the blank decoders in the back of the book to fill out for yourself and to give to others.

Lots to Dot

Reveal a sweet design by connecting the dots, putting the numbers in order from least to greatest.

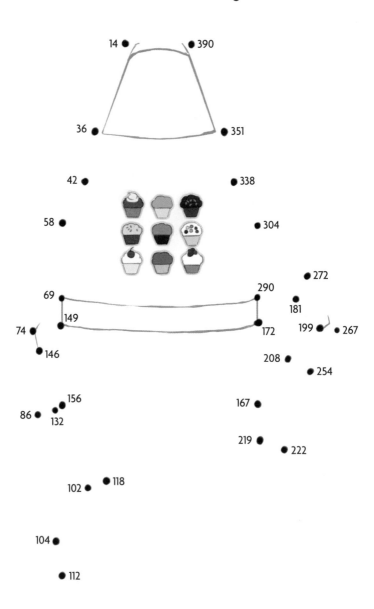

14 ●   ● 390

36 ●   ● 351

42 ●   ● 338

58 ●   ● 304

● 272

69 ●   290 ●

181 ●

149   199 ●   ● 267

74 ●   172 ●

● 146   208 ●

● 254

156 ●   167 ●

86 ●   132

219 ●   ● 222

● 118   102 ●

104 ●

● 112

"Hairbrained" Teasers

**Use your noggin to solve these bobby pin problems
without rearranging the pieces.**

1. Remove 6 bobby pins and leave 9.

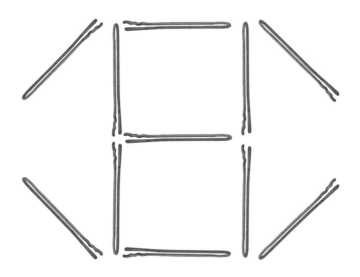

2. Remove 3 bobby pins and leave 4.

Sock Stock

Someone has just delivered boxes upon boxes of socks to Twinkly Toes. The number of sock pairs is written on each box. Using multiplication, figure out how many pairs of each sock style were delivered.

Bonus question: How many total pairs of socks are there? _____

9

11

11

9

6

7

3

2

9

9

9

3

9

7

11

14

11

6

9

9

7

3

3

11

11

9

9

3

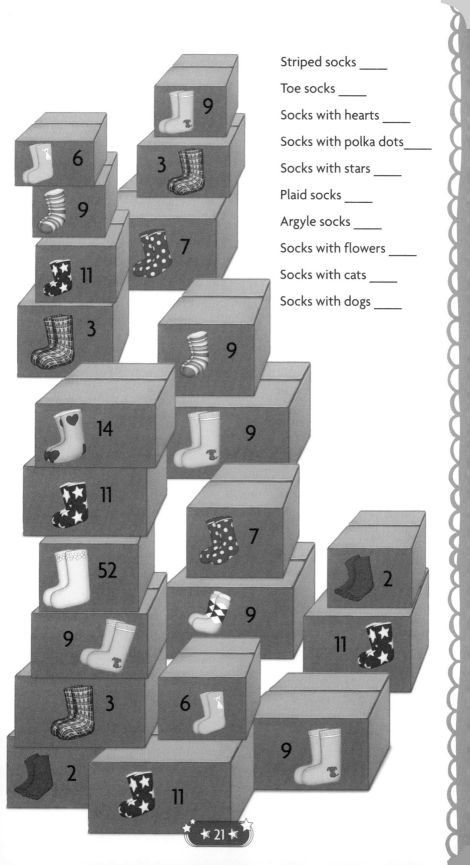

Striped socks ____
Toe socks ____
Socks with hearts ____
Socks with polka dots____
Socks with stars ____
Plaid socks ____
Argyle socks ____
Socks with flowers ____
Socks with cats ____
Socks with dogs ____

Purse Prediction

Impress your friends with this amazing trick!

Beforehand

Multiply the current year by 2. If the year is 2012, your answer will be 4,024. Write this number on a slip of paper and close it inside a small purse.

Do the trick!

1. Find a friend or family member. Announce that you have predicted her magic number and have closed it inside a small purse.
2. Ask your volunteer to write down the age that she will be at the end of this year. Then ask her to write down the year she was born.
3. Now ask your volunteer to write down the age her sibling or parent will be at the end of this year and the year that person was born.
4. Ask the volunteer to add the 4 numbers together carefully.
5. If the person adds correctly, her number will match the number you wrote down. Open the purse and shock her with your magic number!

How it works: If your magic feat goes correctly, every person's answer will always be twice the current year.

Slumber Savings

★ Isabel was invited to a birthday slumber party for Riley. At Pajama Jam, Isabel is looking for a new pair of PJ's to wear to the party as well as a cute gift for Riley. Isabel spends exactly $36.62. Circle the three items that she buys.

$11.89

$13.73

$6.80

$16.82

$10.34

$17.24

$22.41

$8.12

SHAMPOO

$19.66

$42

$12.55

Messy Maze

The new secondhand store is a mess! The only way to get through this mess is with a little math. Help Isabel find a path through the piles of clothes. Solve the addition and subtraction problems and then shade in the correct answers to find the path.

1. 462
    -329
    _____

2. 233
    $+195$
    _____

3. 334
    -289
    _____

4. 568
    $+379$
    _____

5. 504
    -233
    _____

6. 647
    $+279$
    _____

7. 562
    -398
    _____

8. 102
    $+424$
    _____

9. 876
    -525
    _____

10. 775
     $+196$
     _____

11. 420
     -132
     _____

12. 442
     $+259$
     _____

13. 310
     $+647$
     _____

791	428	23
133	38	947

141	45	428	54	624
623	947	326	351	227
189	271	737	211	42
164	926	368	288	957
526	960	552	401	354
351	971	288	701	579
701	183	322	957	337

623	337	54
947	901	405
189	38	125
411	288	957
791	211	204
50	405	337

Funny Fashion

Isabel has a funny joke for you. Solve each multiplication problem and match the answers with the letters to fill in the blanks.

63	140	60	144	90	98	128	88	45
A	D	E	G	H	N	O	U	Y

What did the hat rack say to the hat?

15	32	11
x 3	x 4	x 8

24	64
x 6	x 2

8	14
x 16	x 7

21
x 3

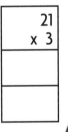

10	12	9	20
x 9	x 5	x 7	x 7

Sequence Sequins

Find the missing number in each sequence
and write it in the blank sequin.

Bracelet Bonanza

Isabel's jewelry box is overflowing, and she wants to donate some of her bracelets to the Care and Share Clothing Drive. Add the numbers inside each bracelet. If the sum is odd, Isabel will donate the bracelet. If the sum is even, she'll keep it. Which bracelets will Isabel give away?

1. 17 4

2. 12 3

3. 6 24

4. 3 48

5. 4 38

6. 12 18

7. 13 87

8. 33 77

9. 22 43

10. 46 54

Loads of Leggings

Neely needs help dividing the mess of leggings into more store bins. Count the leggings. Then figure out how many leggings will fit evenly into 2 bins, 3 bins, and 4 bins.

Total leggings = _____

2 bins = _____   3 bins = _____   4 bins = _____

Earring Organizer

Help Isabel organize her earrings on these racks. In each problem, each column, row, and diagonal adds up to the same number. Fill in the missing digits for each square. There's only one perfect way to arrange these—no number will appear more than once in a problem.

= 0   = 1   = 2   = 3

= 4   = 5   = 6   = 7

= 8   = 9   = 10   = 11

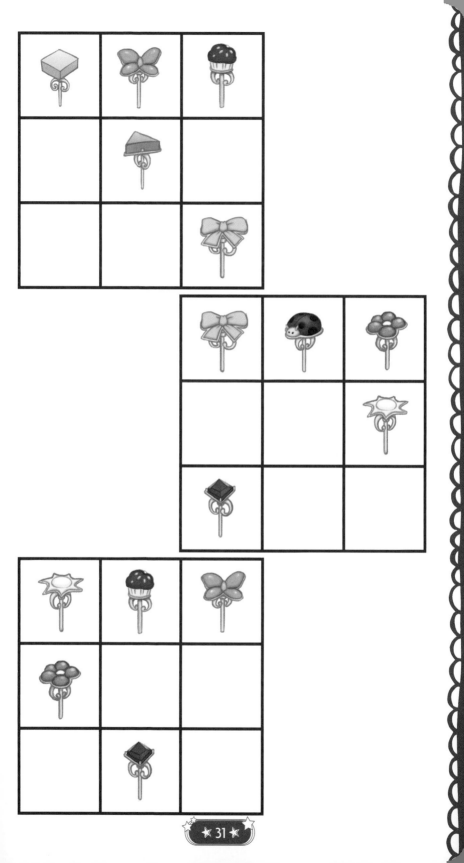

Sweater Stacks

For each stack, count the number of sweaters and round that number up or down to a number ending in 0 or 5.

2. _____ _____
Actual Rounded

3. _____ _____
Actual Rounded

1. _____ _____
Actual Rounded

4. _____ _____
Actual Rounded

5. _____ _____
Actual Rounded

6. _____ _____
Actual Rounded

7. _____ _____
Actual Rounded

8. _____ _____
Actual Rounded

Cap Combine

Isabel is looking for a new winter hat. Which hat does she pick?
To find out, add together the numbers in each hat and
circle the hat that equals an odd number.

1. 18 14 2 Total =

2. 54 3 17 Total =

3. 35 25 12 Total =

4. 42 33 11 Total =

5. 7 63 13 Total =

6. 26 14 2 Total =

Solve the problems
by combining two
easier numbers first.
Then add the
third number.

Perfect Gift Search

**Isabel wants to buy Shelby, Neely, and Amber matching
thank-you gifts at Casual Closet. She needs to buy gift bags, too.**

For all of the items, Isabel wants to spend as close to $20 as
she can without going over. If Isabel buys one gift and one gift bag
for each person, what gift does she choose?

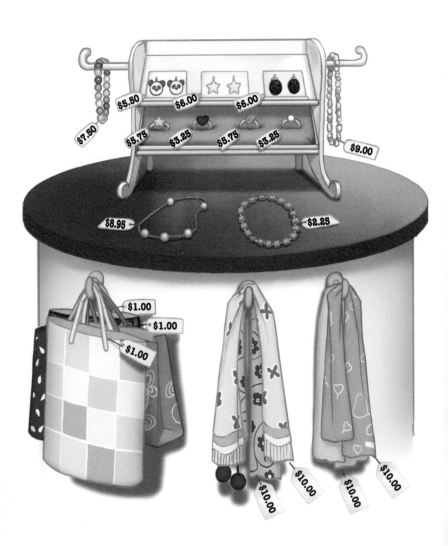

Add up these items based on the prices from the previous page:

TOTAL: $

TOTAL: $

TOTAL: $

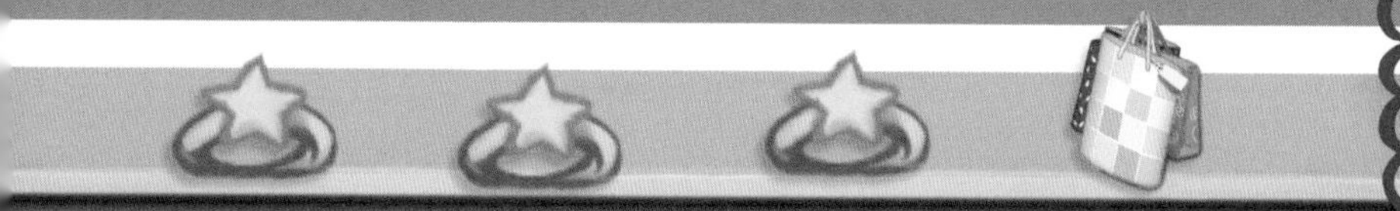

TOTAL: $

TOTAL: $

★ 35 ★

Formal Affair

Glittering Gown is having a "buy one, get one half off" sale!

Divide the price of the second dress in half, and add up how much the pair of dresses will cost. Then add up how much each pair of girls can spend. Write in the pair of girls under the pair of dresses they buy. The amounts will be exact.

1.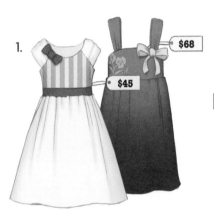

2.

3.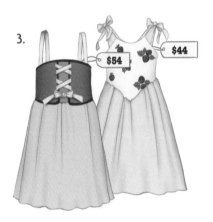

4.

Pair A	**Pair C**
Emmy has $32; Neely has $33.	Logan has $35; Shelby has $41.
Pair B	**Pair D**
Amber has $40; Isabel has $39.	Paige has $51; Riley has $49.

Shopping Bag Bundle

A new batch of 24 clear bags came into Casual Closet, and Isabel needs help finding them. Write down the 4 letters that make up each rectangular shopping bag.

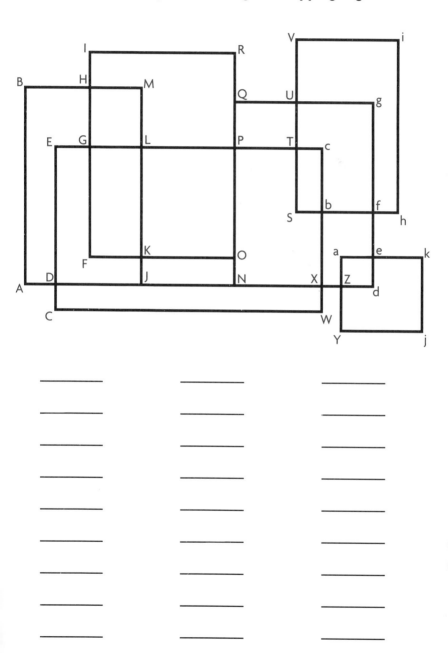

Hidden Accessories

Solve these problems and then use the colors to fill in the areas on the next page.

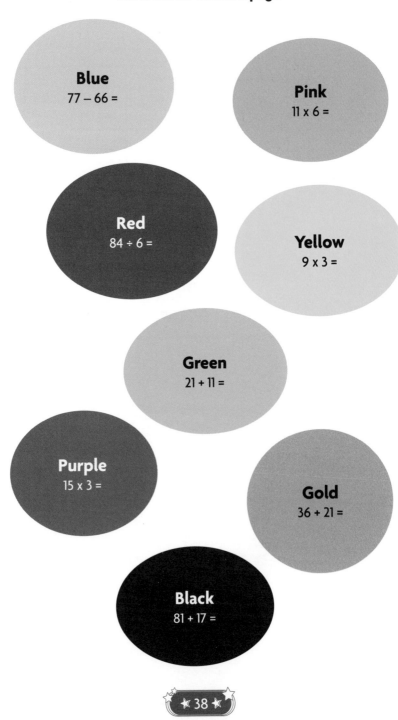

Blue
77 − 66 =

Pink
11 x 6 =

Red
84 ÷ 6 =

Yellow
9 x 3 =

Green
21 + 11 =

Purple
15 x 3 =

Gold
36 + 21 =

Black
81 + 17 =

Good Deal

Not every sale is what it seems. Put your knowledge of fractions and percentages to the test. Number each rack of clothing in order from 1 to 6, with 1 being the least expensive item of clothing in the store and 6 being the most expensive. Write the number on the store sign.

$30
1/2
OFF

$12
BUY 1
GET 2ND
HALF OFF

$32
75% OFF

Hair Affair

Isabel wants to buy a matching headband and hair elastic set, but she can spend only $7 or less. Add up the costs of both pieces in each set and see which set she can buy.

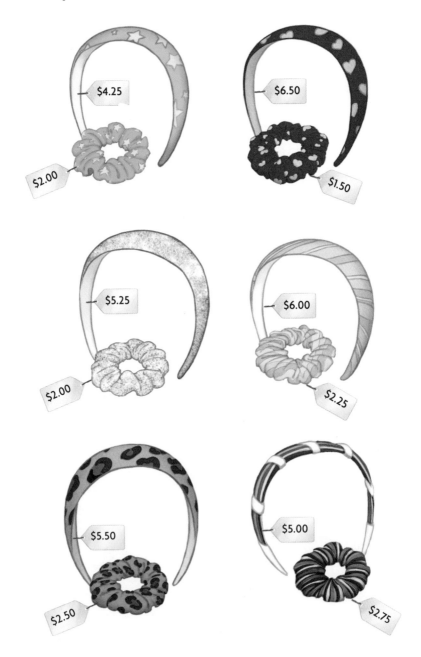

$4.25

$2.00

$6.50

$1.50

$5.25

$2.00

$6.00

$2.25

$5.50

$2.50

$5.00

$2.75

Quick Change

While cleaning her closet, Isabel finds $2.50 in the pocket of her coat and $1.25 in the pocket of her jeans. Circle the pile with the correct amount of money that Isabel can put in her piggy bank.

1.

2.

3.

4.

Fashion Fractions

Casual Closet is bursting with fractions. Look at the store displays to figure out the fractions. The first one is done for you.

1. Blue dresses
What fraction of the dresses are blue? _3/4_

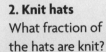

2. Knit hats
What fraction of the hats are knit?

_____

3. Star rings
What fraction of the rings have stars?

_____

4. Pink pants
What fraction of the pants are pink? _____

5. Green socks
What fraction of the sock pairs are green? _____

6. Heart T-shirts
What fraction of the T-shirts have hearts? _____

7. Purple barrettes
What fraction of the barrettes are purple?

_____

8. Beaded bracelets
What fraction of the bracelets are beaded?

_____

Spending Stumpers

Isabel and her friends need help solving multiplication problems on the spot as they browse their favorite stores.

1. Shelby wants to buy 3 flavors of lip gloss. If they cost $1.25 each, how much will she spend?

_____

2. At Casual Closet, Neely spots 4 pretty barrettes that will keep her hair back during dance class. They're $2 each. How much will it cost to buy them all?

_____

3. Amber is saving to buy 2 new pairs of pants. They each cost $7.25. How much money will she need to save?

_____

4. Paige has $10 to spend. How many pairs of sunglasses can she buy if they cost $2.50 each?

_____

5. Riley needs to buy some soccer accessories at Girl Gear. The shin guards, socks, and shorts are all on sale for $5 each. If she buys 1 pair of shin guards, 2 pairs of socks, and 2 pairs of shorts, how much money will she spend?

_____

6. Emmy finds some mix-and-match swimsuits that she loves. If she buys 2 tops and 2 bottoms, how many swimsuit combinations can she make?

_____

7. Logan is shopping for party favors for her upcoming birthday. She wants to buy bracelets for her 12 guests. The bracelets come in sets of 4 that cost $3.25 each. How much will she spend?

_____

8. Isabel has $10 to spend, but she needs to save $4 for the movies tonight. How many rings can she buy if they cost $2 each?

_____

Pendant Count

Place every even number from 2 to 18 in the necklace pendant so that the numbers in any straight line add up to 30.

2　4　6　8　~~10~~　12　14　16　18

Shoe Pair-Up

It's time for new shoes! Isabel and her friends have exact change to pay for their purchases. Draw a line from the pair of shoes to the correct pile of money.

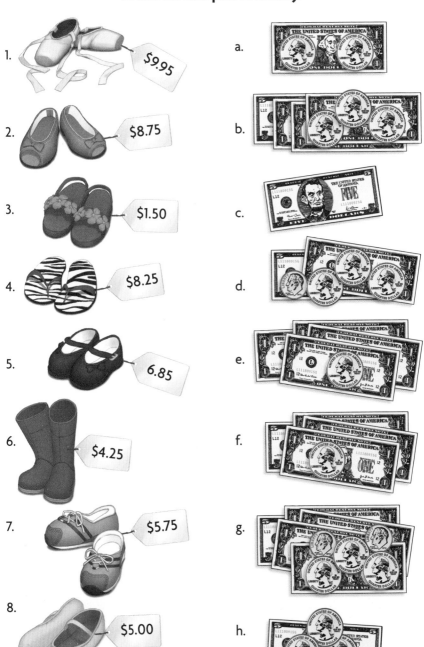

1. $9.95

2. $8.75

3. $1.50

4. $8.25

5. 6.85

6. $4.25

7. $5.75

8. $5.00

a.

b.

c.

d.

e.

f.

g.

h.

Fashion Frames

Using the grid, write down both numbers and solve the equation.
The first one is done for you.

	Left Side Number	Top Number	Total

1. __10__ − __3__ = __7__

2. _____ + _____ = _____

3. _____ + _____ = _____

4. _____ x _____ = _____

5. _____ − _____ = _____

6. _____ + _____ = _____

7. _____ x _____ = _____

8. _____ ÷ _____ = _____

9. _____ − _____ = _____

10. _____ x _____ = _____

Charity Knitting

Neely is planning to knit scarves and to donate them to a winter clothing drive. She needs to buy a set of knitting needles, a scarf pattern, and 2 balls of yarn. All 4 items together cost exactly $16. Circle the items that Neely will buy.

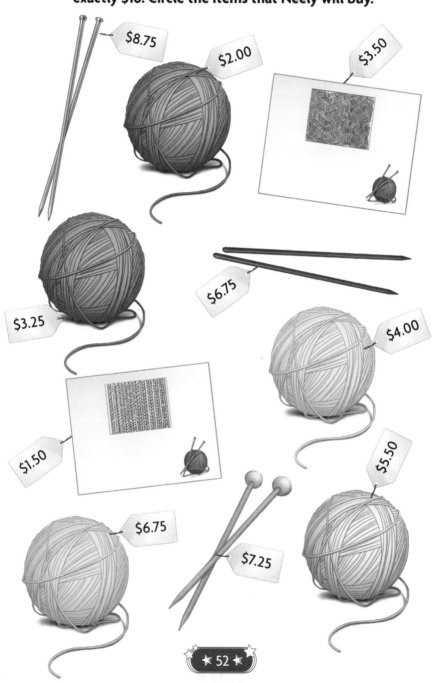

$8.75

$2.00

$3.50

$6.75

$3.25

$4.00

$1.50

$6.75

$7.25

$5.50

Budget Busters

Isabel and her friends have a fun-filled day planned. Match each girl to the appropriate activity based on the dollar amount and time she has to spend. Use only one girl for each activity.

Neely
3 hours
$10.00

Isabel
3 hours
$4.00

Shelby
1.5 hours
$5.00

Amber
2 hours
$8.00

Riley
4 hours
$4.50

Fashion Show
2 hours
$4.00

Crochet Class
2 hours
$10.00

Manicure
1 hour 15 minutes
$7.00

French Braid Demo
1 hour 30 minutes
$5.00

Fashion Exhibit
3 hours 5 minutes
$1.50

_____

_____

_____

_____

_____

Exact Change

There is a long line of customers waiting to buy jewelry at Neely's jewelry-making stand. Each person is spending a different amount, but each is paying with a $20 bill. Draw a line to connect the price tag with the exact change Neely should give back.

$19.50

$18.99

$5.75

$16.40

$3.34

$10.00

Twisted Tags

Connect the even-numbered price tags to make your way through the price tag maze.

Start

$8	$19	$27	$67	$55	$49
$16	$100	$24	$101	$39	$29
$5	$17	$44	$33	$45	$77
$51	$89	$68	$4	$90	$31
$191	$75	$15	$23	$72	$283
$86	$54	$36	$12	$6	$7
$30	$11	$37	$41	$65	$9
$2	$122	$56	$22	$43	$13
$59	$333	$1	$246	$66	$76

Finish

Design Dots

Count by threes to connect the dots
and design a look with spirit.

Math Makeover

These crazy styles need a makeover! Simplify the looks by changing the addition problems into multiplication problems. Then solve the problems.

3 + 3
3 + 3 +

3 x 4 = 12

6 + 6 + 6 + 6 + 6

6 x ☐ = ☐

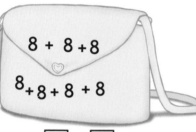

8 + 8 + 8
8 + 8 + 8 + 8

8 x ☐ = ☐

1 + 1 + 1 + 1
1 + 1 + 1 + 1

1 x ☐ = ☐

In 3 + 3 + 3 + 3, the number 3 appears 4 times. That's why 3 x 4 equals the same answer: 12.

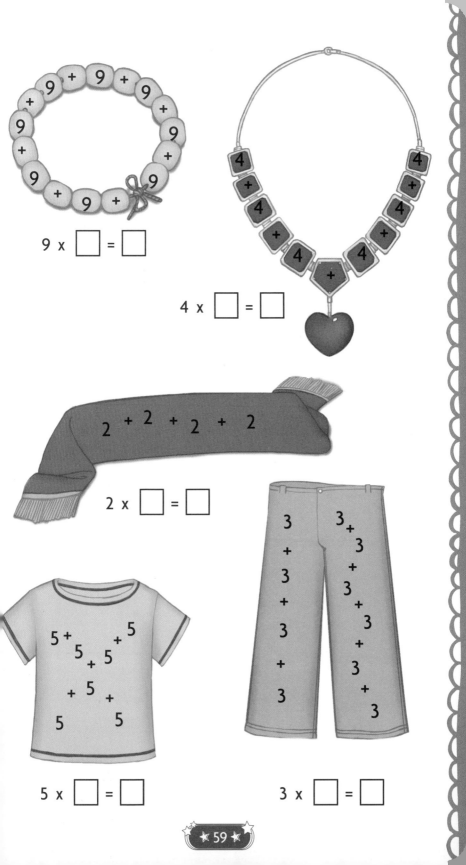

9 x ☐ = ☐

4 x ☐ = ☐

2 x ☐ = ☐

5 x ☐ = ☐

3 x ☐ = ☐

Clothing Conundrum

Patterns galore! Isabel needs help clearing some clutter.
Look at Isabel's closet to answer the following questions.

1. What fraction of Isabel's clothes are striped?

_____

2. Which print does Isabel have more of—stripes or dots?

_____

3. How many different outfits can Isabel make with these clothes?

_____

4. If Isabel donated half of her dot clothes and half of her solid-colored clothes to charity, how many pieces of clothing would she have left?

_____

Bead Blanks

Fill in the string of beads with the correct addition sign or subtraction sign. Colored beads between equations will be blank.

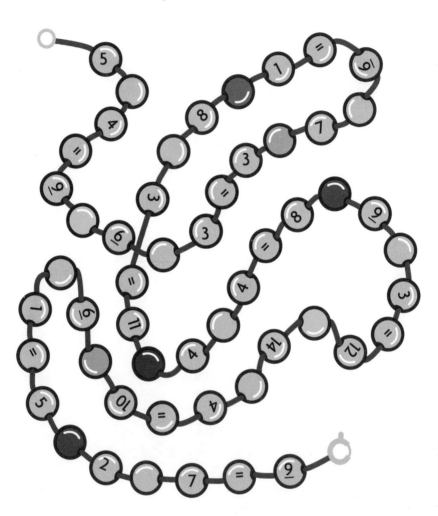

It All Adds Up

Isabel and Neely have been making bracelets on their own but want to sell them together at the craft show. Neely thinks that she has made the same number of bracelets as Isabel, but Isabel is not so sure. Circle the name of the person who is correct.

Market Maze

Isabel has had a busy day walking around the Market.
Solve the problems and match the answers to the tent numbers
to help you see all the places she visited.

1. $4 \times 7 =$ 2. $9 \times 2 =$ 3. $7 \times 8 =$

4. $3 \times 4 =$ 5. $9 \times 9 =$

Charming Charms 12

Terrific Tees 28

Care and Share 15

Rings 'n' Things 39

Glam Glasses 48

Spectacular Scarves 56

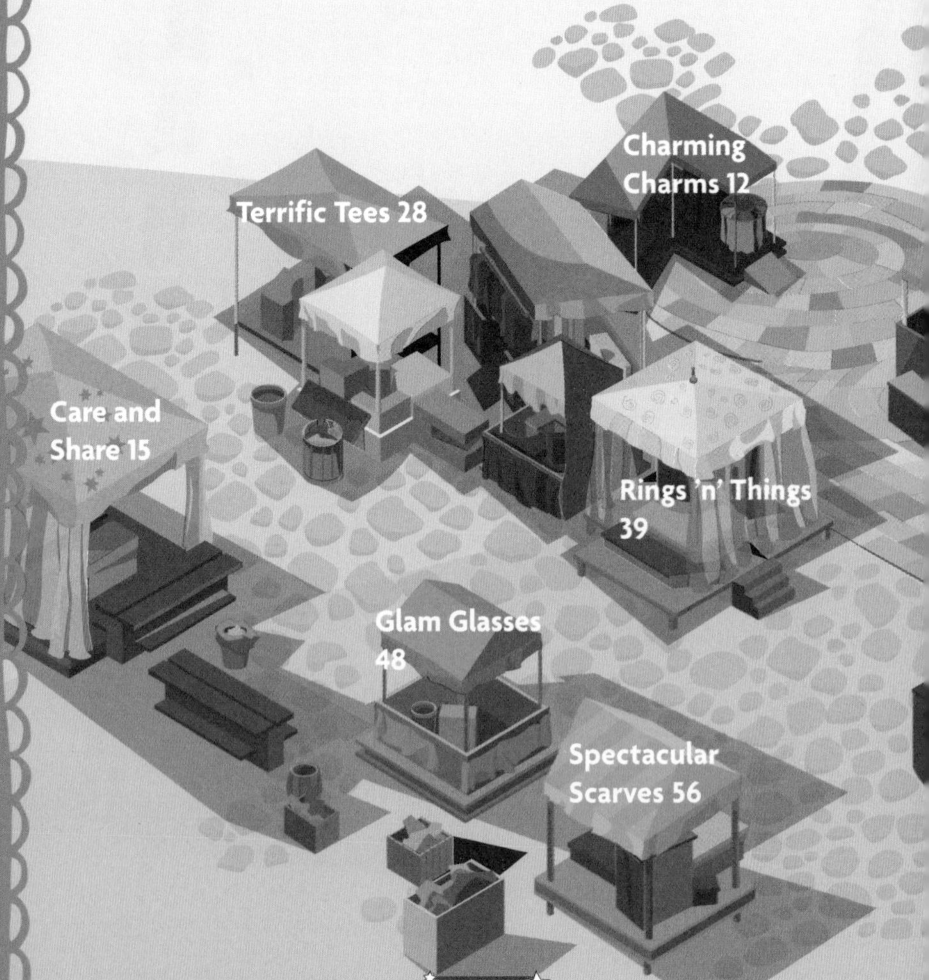

Sound Stage 72

Super Shoes 8

Bright Kites 18

retty Purses
3

Excellent Earrings
81

Pet Sets 50

Handmade
Hats 92

★ ★ 65 ★ ★

Message Mix-Up

Isabel has a message for you. Write the fractions in order from smallest to largest. Then fill in their corresponding letters below to solve the special message from Isabel.

¹⁄₁₆ = I	⅔ = U
1¾ = E	½ = O
⅞ = T	1 = Y
⅛ = L	¾ = S
⅜ = K	¹¹⁄₁₆ = R

_ _ _i _ _e

y_ _ _ _ _ _ _l _ !

Jewelry Palooza

Isabel, Paige, Neely, and Logan each have $15.00 to spend at the market's jewelry tent. Use the grid below to fill in their purchases and find out **who has $4.00 left** to buy a smoothie.

- Isabel, Neely, and Logan each buy a pair of matching heart earrings for $4.75.

- Paige finds a pair of panda earrings for $5.00 that she loves.

- Isabel and Logan each buy a necklace for an aunt. Necklaces cost 2 for $12.00.

- Neely buys a purple bracelet for $5.75, while Paige finds a black-and-white dot bracelet on sale for $4.25.

- Logan and Neely pick out key chains. Key chains cost 2 for $1, and each girl buys one.

- Paige and Isabel split the cost of a $6.50 watch to give as a gift to Logan.

| Amount Spent | | | |
	Purchases	Purchases	Purchases	Money left over
Isabel	$4.75			
Paige				
Neely	$4.75			
Logan	$4.75			

Purchase Path

Use math to help Isabel find her way to her great purchases.
Solve the multiplication and division problems, and then
shade in the correct answers to find the path.

1.   54
    ÷ 9

2.   70
    x 3

3.   48
    ÷ 12

4.   11
    x 11

5.   136
    ÷ 8

6.   15
    x 12

7.   81
    ÷ 9

8.   72
    x 9

9.   64
    ÷ 8

10.   59
    x 15

11. 1,010
    ÷ 10

12.   12
    x 12

13.   115
    ÷ 5

14.   45
    x 6

15.   77
    ÷ 11

16.   122
    x 2

17.   510
    ÷ 5

18.   56
    x 12

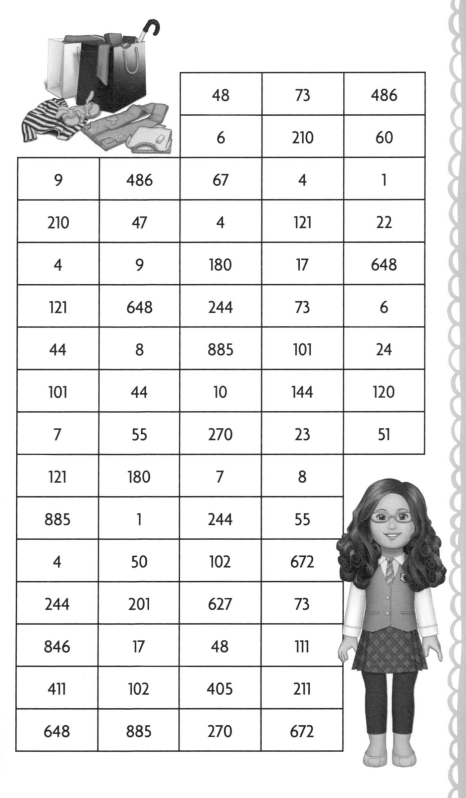

		48	73	486
		6	210	60
9	486	67	4	1
210	47	4	121	22
4	9	180	17	648
121	648	244	73	6
44	8	885	101	24
101	44	10	144	120
7	55	270	23	51
121	180	7	8	
885	1	244	55	
4	50	102	672	
244	201	627	73	
846	17	48	111	
411	102	405	211	
648	885	270	672	

Store Secret

Solve these problems, then use the answers to color in the numbers and reveal a hidden message.

24 = pink   36 = purple   48 = green

60 = blue   72 = yellow

a.   8 x 3 = _____

b.   12 x 3 = _____

c.   192 ÷ 4 = _____

d.   12 x 2 = _____

e.   3 x 20 = _____

f.   6 x 10 = _____

g.   9 x 4 = _____

h.   12 x 6 = _____

i.   12 x 4 = _____

j.   9 x 8 = _____

k.   18 x 2 = _____

l.   96 ÷ 2 = _____

m.   180 ÷ 5 = _____

n.   5 x 12 = _____

o.   288 ÷ 4 = _____

p.   96 ÷ 4 = _____

q.   144 ÷ 3 = _____

r.   36 x 2 = _____

s.   16 x 3 = _____

t.   48 ÷ 2 = _____

u.   15 x 4 = _____

v.   18 x 4 = _____

w.   360 ÷ 5 = _____

x.   240 ÷ 4 = _____

y.   6 x 6 = _____

z.   72 ÷ 3 = _____

Answers

Bead Bins
Page 11

```
4 + 3 + 8
+   +   +
9 + 5 + 1
+   +   +
2 + 7 + 6
```

Color Coordinated
Pages 12 & 13

a. 6 x 2 = 12
b. 2 x 3 = 6
c. 5 x 4 = 20
d. 12 x 2 = 24
e. 3 x 2 = 6
f. 48 ÷ 2 = 24
g. 10 x 4 = 40
h. 36 ÷ 6 = 6
i. 8 x 5 = 40
j. 10 x 2 = 20
k. 20 x 2 = 40
l. 4 x 3 = 12
m. 8 x 3 = 24

Clothing Code
Pages 14 & 15

A	B	C	D	E	F	G	H	I	J	K	L	M
17	1	2	13	4	18	8	23	3	19	9	7	14

N	O	P	Q	R	S	T	U	V	W	X	Y	Z
6	16	10	25	21	26	5	11	24	12	20	15	22

A. 17	**B.** 1	**C.** 2
D. 13	**E.** 4	**F.** 18
G. 8	**H.** 23	**I.** 3
J. 19	**K.** 9	**L.** 7
M. 14	**N.** 6	**O.** 16
P. 10	**Q.** 25	**R.** 21
S. 26	**T.** 5	**U.** 11
V. 24	**W.** 12	**X.** 20
Y. 15	**Z.** 22	

Page 16

1. nice belt
2. sneakers
3. a shirt
4. a dog
5. clogs
6. open-toad
7. a buccaneer

Lots to Dot
Page 18

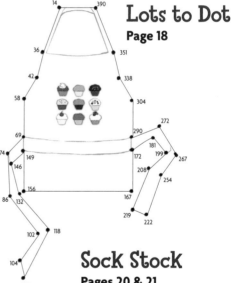

"Hairbrained" Teasers Page 19

1.  (The number nine)

2. (The roman numeral four)

Sock Stock
Pages 20 & 21

Striped socks: 54 pairs
Toe socks: 6 pairs
Socks with hearts: 28 pairs
Socks with polka dots: 35 pairs
Socks with stars: 110 pairs
Plaid socks: 24 pairs
Argyle socks: 27 pairs
Socks with flowers: 52 pairs
Socks with cats: 24 pairs
Socks with dogs: 63 pairs
Bonus answer: 423 pairs

Slumber Savings
Page 23

slippers: $12.55
snowflake pajama pants: $13.73
long-sleeve pajama shirt: $10.34

Funny Fashion Page 26

15 x 3	32 x 4	11 x 8
45	128	88
Y	O	U

24 x 6	64 x 2
144	128
G	O

8 x 16	14 x 7
128	98
O	N

21 x 3
63
A

10 x 9	12 x 5	9 x 7	20 x 7
90	60	63	140
H	E	A	D

Sequence Sequins
Page 27

pink dress: 10 (every third number is skipped)
green dress: 6 (count by 3s)
lavender purse: 10 (count by 2s)
green purse: 15 (count by 10s)
blue belt: 110 (count by 11s)
coral belt: 35 (count by 7s)

Bracelet Bonanza
Page 28

1. 21
2. 15
3. 30
4. 51
5. 42
6. 30
7. 100
8. 110
9. 65
10. 100

Isabel will give away bracelets 1, 2, 4, and 9.

Loads of Leggings
Page 29

Total number of leggings in the bin: 24
2 bins: 12 per bin
3 bins: 8 per bin
4 bins: 6 per bin

Messy Maze Pages 24 & 25

	791	428	23	
	133	38	947	
141	45	428	54	624
623	947	326	351	227
189	271	737	211	42
164	926	368	288	957
526	960	552	401	354
351	971	288	701	579
701	183	322	957	337
623	337	54		
947	901	405		
189	38	125		
411	288	957		
791	211	204		
50	405	337		

1. 133
2. 428
3. 45
4. 947
5. 271
6. 926
7. 164
8. 526
9. 351
10. 971
11. 288
12. 701
13. 957

Earring Organizer
Pages 30 & 31

	8	0
3	2	

2	6	
	4	5

	7	11
8		4

Sweater Stacks

Page 32

1. Actual 14   Rounded 15
2. Actual 4   Rounded 5
3. Actual 11   Rounded 10
4. Actual 8   Rounded 10
5. Actual 2   Rounded 0
6. Actual 19   Rounded 20
7. Actual 16   Rounded 15
8. Actual 12   Rounded 10

Perfect Gift Search

Pages 34 & 35

3 beaded bracelets and 3 gift bags: $9.75

3 shooting star earring pairs and 3 gift bags: $21.00

3 heart rings and 3 gift bags: $12.75

3 shooting star rings and 3 gift bags: $20.25

3 panda earring pairs and 3 gift bags: $19.50

Isabel buys 3 panda earring pairs and 3 gift bags for $19.50.

Shopping Bag Bundle

Page 37

1. ABMJ
2. DEPN
3. DEPN
4. DELJ
5. DEcX
6. FGLK
7. FGPO
8. FHMK
9. FIRO
10. GHML
11. GIRP
12. JKON
13. JLPN
14. JLCX
15. KLPO
16. NPcX
17. NQgd
18. PQUT
19. STcb
20. SUgf
21. SVih
22. Xbfd
23. Yakj
24. Zaed
25. CEcW

Cap Combine

Page 33

1. 34   4. 86
2. 74   5. 83
3. 72   6. 42

Isabel buys hat 5.

Formal Affair

Page 36

Gown Pair 1—Pair B (total $79)

Gown Pair 2—Pair D (total $100)

Gown Pair 3—Pair C (total $76)

Gown Pair 4—Pair A (total $65)

Hidden Accessories

Pages 38 & 39

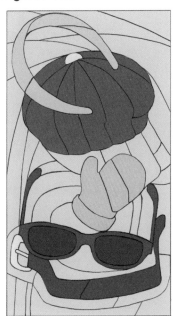

Good Deal Pages 40 & 41

Rack 1: 75% off $32 = $8 per item of clothing

Rack 2: $12 + $6 (1/2 off) = $18 $18/2 = $9 per item of clothing

Rack 3: $16 x 3 = $48 $48/4 = $12 per item of clothing

Rack 4: 50% off $30 = $15 per item of clothing

Rack 5: 20% off $20 = $4 $20 – $4 = $16 per item of clothing

Rack 6: $40/2 = $20 per item of clothing

Hair Affair
Page 42

Star set = $6.25
Heart set = $8.00
Sky blue set = $7.25
Pastel stripe set = $8.25
Leopard print set = $8.00
Rainbow set = $7.75

Isabel can buy the star set.

Spending Stumpers
Pages 46 & 47

1. 3 x $1.25 = $3.75
2. 4 x $2 = $8
3. 2 x $7.25 = $14.50
4. $10 ÷ $2.50 = 4
5. 5 x $5 = $25
6. 2 tops x 2 bottoms = 4
7. 3 x $3.25 = $9.75
8. $10 − $4 = $6, $6 ÷ $2 = 3

Shoe Pair-Up Page 49

1. g. $9.95   5. d. $6.85
2. b. $8.75   6. e. $4.25
3. a. $1.50   7. h. $5.75
4. f. $8.25   8. c. $5.00

Fashion Frames
Pages 50 & 51

1. 10−3=7   6. 13+6=19
2. 4+10=14   7. 5x2=10
3. 7+13=20   8. 9÷3=3
4. 8x7=56   9. 11−7=4
5. 15−10=5   10. 12x5=60

Charity Knitting
Page 52

wooden needles set: $7.25
purple pattern: $3.50
red yarn: $3.25
purple yarn: $2.00

Budget Busters
Page 53

Fashion Show: Isabel
Crochet Class: Neely
Manicure: Amber
French Braid Demo: Shelby
Fashion Exhibit: Riley

Quick Change
Page 43

2. $3.75

Fashion Fractions
Pages 44 & 45

1. 3/4   5. 1/4
2. 2/3   6. 5/8
3. 3/8   7. 2/5
4. 1/4   8. 1/3

Pendant Count Page 48

Exact Change Pages 54 & 55

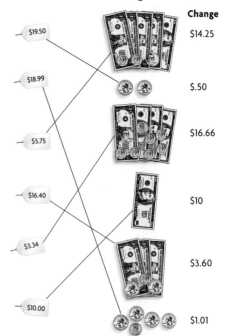

Twisted Tags Page 56

Start						
$9	$19	$27	$67	$55	$49	
$16	$100	$24	$101	$39	$29	
$5	$17	$44	$33	$45	$77	
$51	$89	$68	$4	$90	$31	
$191	$75	$15	$23	$72	$283	
$86	$54	$36	$12	$6	$7	
$30	$11	$37	$41	$65	$9	
$2	$122	$56	$22	$43	$13	
$59	$333	$1	$246	$66	$76	

Finish

Design Dots Page 57

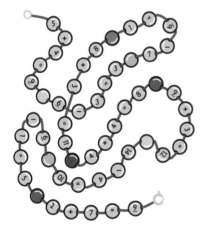

Math Makeover
Pages 58 & 59

Hat: 3 x 4 = 12
Belt: 6 x 5 = 30
Purse: 8 x 7 = 56
Boots: 1 x 6 = 6
Bracelet: 9 x 8 = 72
Necklace: 4 x 6 = 24
Scarf: 2 x 4 = 8
T-shirt: 5 x 7 = 35
Pants: 3 x 10 = 30

Clothing Conundrum Pages 60 & 61

a. 5/13 striped
b. Dots
c. 42 (6 bottoms x 7 tops = 42 combinations)
d. 9 (6 items in Isabel's closet are dotted.
   Half of 6 is 3. 2 items are solid-colored.
   Half of 2 is 1. Together that adds up to 4
   items. There are 13 total items in the closet
   before donation. 13 – 4 = 9

Bead Blanks Page 62

Market Maze Pages 64 & 65

1. 28, Terrific Tees
2. 18, Bright Kites
3. 56, Spectacular Scarves
4. 12, Charming Charms
5. 81, Excellent Earrings

Message Mix-Up Page 66

Message: I like your style!
Fraction order:
I (1/16)
L (1/8)
K (3/8)
O (1/2)
U (2/3)
R (11/16)
S (3/4)
T (7/8)
Y (1)
E (1 3/4)

It All Adds Up
Page 63

Isabel
(Isabel has 36 and
Neely has 34.)

Jewelry Palooza Page 67

	Purchases	Purchases	Purchases	Money left over
	Amount Spent			
Isabel	$4.75	$6.00	$3.25	$1.00
Paige	$5.00	$4.25	$3.25	$2.50
Neely	$4.75	$5.75	$.50	$4.00
Logan	$4.75	$6.00	$.50	$3.75

Purchase Path
Pages 68 & 69

	48	73	486	
	6	210	60	
9	486	67	4	1
210	47	4	121	22
4	9	180	17	648
121	648	244	73	6
44	8	885	101	24
101	44	10	144	120
7	55	270	23	51
121	180	7	8	
885	1	244	55	
4	50	102	672	
244	201	627	73	
846	17	48	111	
411	102	405	211	
648	885	270	672	

1. 6
2. 210
3. 4
4. 121
5. 17
6. 180
7. 9
8. 648
9. 8
10. 885
11. 101
12. 144
13. 23
14. 270
15. 7
16. 244
17. 102
18. 672

Store Secret
Pages 70 & 71

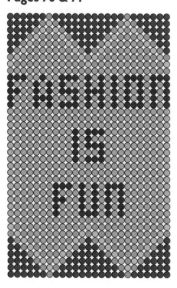

a. 24
b. 36
c. 48
d. 24
e. 60
f. 60
g. 36
h. 72
i. 48
j. 72
k. 36
l. 48
m. 36

n. 60
o. 72
p. 24
q. 48
r. 72
s. 48
t. 24
u. 60
v. 72
w. 72
x. 60
y. 36
z. 24

INNERSTARU.COM

The puzzle fun continues online!

Use the code below for access to
even more puzzles and activities.

Go online to innerstarU.com/puzzle
and enter this code: MATHFASH

Basic System Requirements:
Windows: Internet Explorer 7 or 8, Firefox 2.0+, Google Chrome
Mac: Safari 4.0+
Monitor Resolution: Optimized for 1024 x 768 or larger
Flash Version 10 and high-speed Internet required

Requirements may change. Visit www.innerstarU.com for
full requirements and latest updates.

Important Information:
Recommended for girls 8 and up. American Girl reserves the right
to modify, restrict access to, or discontinue www.innerstarU.com
at any time, in its sole discretion, without prior notice.

Here are some other American Girl books you might like:

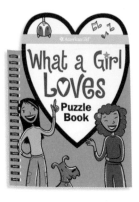

❑ I read it.

❑ I read it.

❑ I read it.

❑ I read it.

❑ I read it.

❑ I read it.

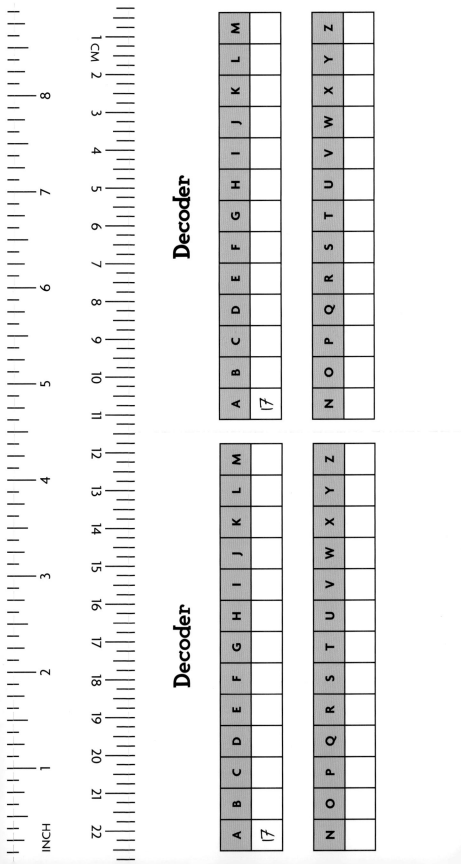

Decoder

A	B	C	D	E	F	G	H	I	J	K	L	M
17												

N	O	P	Q	R	S	T	U	V	W	X	Y	Z

Decoder

A	B	C	D	E	F	G	H	I	J	K	L	M
17												

N	O	P	Q	R	S	T	U	V	W	X	Y	Z

Measurements & Equivalents

1 foot (ft) = 12 inches
1 yard (yd) = 3 feet = 36 inches
1 mile (mi) = 1,760 yards = 5,280 feet
1 tablespoon (T) = 3 teaspoons (t)
1 cup (c) = 16 T = 8 ounces (oz)
1 pint (pt) = 2 c
1 quart (qt) = 2 pt = 4 c = 32 oz
1 gallon (gal) = 4 qt

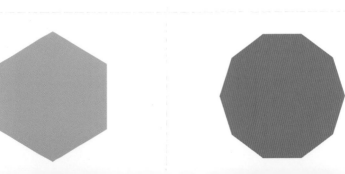

Heptagon	Triangle
Octagon	Rectangle
Nonagon	Pentagon
Decagon	Hexagon